"A Woman's Work is Never Done..."

Embroidery as decorative art was not only useful, but provided an enjoyable break from heavier household tasks. Vintage stitchery designs provide a lovely record of attitudes, humor and current culture from a woman's point of view.

Everyone who is lucky enough to have a small collection of old linens done by mothers or grandmothers feels the hand reaching across the years. These women put a bit of themselves in with the stitches and would be delighted to see the revival of interest in what they had done.

The current numbers of women collecting embroidered items is continually growing. Women are also taking up the art of embroidery itself.

Nothing makes one feel closer to those who went before than to sit down with an embroidery hoop, some floss, and a picture of a dancing vegetable stamped on a kitchen towel. The humor and whimsy which show up in homespun designs around the house are still relevant and still bring out a smile.

This book is a collection of "Vintage Home" designs, often tongue-in-cheek, that were used on towels, pillows, curtains, and whatever from the 1920's through the 1950's.

They'll give you the chance to walk down memory lane and stitch up your own batch of towels with animated pots and pans, housewives doing chores, husbands getting in the way, and lastly, a touch of the romance that was behind the setting up of households down through the decades.

Pick your favorites and start stitching today!

'Woman's Work' Pillow pattern on pages 20-21.

Quite a feat to use a dish
To tighten up your thighs!
Yet modern girls will find a way -
they know how to compromise!

'China' Exercising Pillow pattern on page 22.
'China' Dancing Pillow pattern on page 23.

1900 - 1920 - Housework was represented by the utensils used. Sober dishes, brooms, and silverware were found throughout the catalogs. Realistic depiction of household items: glassware, china, pots and pans. A few sunbonnets at work can be found. Floral and highly stylized nouveau designs are used extensively.

1920 - 1930 - This is the decade the vegetables began to dance. Animated utensils and busy fruit began to show up more and more. The roaring twenties was also obvious in the images of housewives and "modern" girls that began to be used. Florals, especially baskets, were still extremely popular and were available in every possible variation of design and color.

1930 - 1940 - Women began to laugh at their chores. Humorous dish towel themes began to pop up. Women, usually coquettish and pretty, decorated many towels - doing their daily chores, always on the correct day. Southern belles and elegant ladies were very prevalent. Florals held their own and still were found throughout catalogs. Depictions of black women and servants began to be seen.

1940 - 1950 - The women begin to become more self-assured in their depictions. Catalogs were generally smaller during the war years due to rationing and the exodus of women into factories for war work. The second half of the decade still showed women poking fun at themselves and their husbands as they returned to more traditional roles after the war. Animated utensils and singing vegetables are still popular as are floral designs. Not as many belles are seen and the black stereotypes begin to fade by the end of the decade.

1950 - 1960 - The decline in popularity of embroidery leads to a decline of themes. Housewives are still depicted and humorous jabs between husbands and wives show up. Graceful, stylized girls with flowing hair abound. Flowers make up a lot of designs. Some modern culture creeps in, such as astronauts, spaceships, television and televison characters.

Lady in a Bowl Pillow pattern on page 24.
Serving Cake Pillow pattern on page 25.

1960 - 1990 - A very limited set of designs is available to stitchers. Towels are still popular but they are sometimes outlined in paint rather than stitched. Beginning in the late 1970's and into the 1980's there is a revival of interest in the leisure arts, including needlework. A few core catalogs (Herrschners, Aunt Martha, etc.) still offer towels.

1990 - The growth in quilting, cross stitch, and vintage linen collecting leads to a growing interest in recreating old patterns and embroidery techniques. Books, patterns, and transfers - both old and new- are available to those interested in creating their own vintage and heirloom linens to pass on to the next generation.

Work, Work, Work...

Housework never ended, we're still at it. The chores and tasks depicted in many of the designs shown here have changed a bit over the years.

The tamer versions of women found on the towels done in the Twenties become the coquettish ladies of the Thirties and the Rosie Riveters of the Forties. Few of us use dishes as exercise equipment, but the spirit of the Forties women shows their can-do attitude.

Housewives at their chores was an extremely popular theme through the decades. Available on pre-stamped linens, in kits, and ready to iron-on; these designs were found in great variety.

Monday is for laundry
Come wind or rain or shine.
Tuesday's chore of ironing
Can't be far behind.

Laundry on a Windy Day

The girl fighting to hang her wash was a style popular in the Thirties and Forties. Graceful lines and lithe figures were common depictions. Also popular was the use of words to form items in the picture.

Pattern on page 26 and on pages 28-29.

Laundry List

Laundry was one of the household chores that definitely needed a touch of color and a bit of stitchery to lend a little gaiety to the affair.

Decorated laundry bags were one way to put a happy face on a tedious task.

Washing Blues

This laundry maid comes straight out of the Forties. The long graceful arms are a dead giveaway, as is the slender waist and the WWII hairdo. The touch of blue tinting adds a perfect balance to the long wind-blown lines.

Pattern on pages 30-31.

Dirty Bird

Wherever you found embroidery in the Forties, the bluebird was not far behind. The bird was a great favorite of needlewomen of the period and served as a symbol of happiness. It does its job on this adorable laundry apron.
Pattern on page 39.

Bonnet Babe with Laundry

Bonnet ladies were a perpetual favorite on all types of linen, why not the laundry bag? This lady was ready stamped and tinted and was just waiting to have her stitching done.
Pattern on page 27.

I WOKE
AND FOUND
THAT
LIFE
WAS
DUTY

1700s - Like a sailor's compass or an artist's brush, needles & pins were once precious tools. • Too valuable to waste or lose, sewing items were kept in chatelaines, often made to fold entire mending kits, including scissors, thimble and even magnifier into a tiny space. • Highly decorated chatelaines were fashionable accessories for respectable ladies for well over 100 years.

Mammy with Cake Pillow patterns on pages 42-43.

"I Awoke and Found That Life Was Duty" Pillow patterns on pages 40-41.

Four Dish Towel patterns on pages 44-47.

A Helping Hand

Who wouldn't want a helping hand when digging into housework? While maids are not as common or affordable today, one can still dream. Maybe you will enjoy stitching up one or two of your own.

Maids and Mammy

Maids, servants, and butlers were all common images used on linens. Early on, these were a more realistic version. Starting in the Thirties, these helpers become more fanciful, looking both busier and happier with their tasks.

Black servants and Mammies began showing up in the Twenties and lasted through the late Forties for the most part.

Ladies at Home

The daily chores that make a house a home are so very important. These towels celebrate the stitcher's appreciation of a job done well.

The "bonnet" girl was popular in all its various renditions. This cheerful adaptation is from the Forties. What gives it away is the detail and sense of activity it invokes.
Towel patterns on pages 62-67

Kitchen Mates

The sugar and creamer are perfectly at home on this set of towels. Their romance jumps from towel to towel straight into family life.
Towel patterns on pages 58-61.

An Apple a Day

When apples court, romance can never be far behind.

This fruit combo is a perfect example of the tongue-in-cheek designs from the Thirties. The Depression was a tough time. One way to deal with adversity is humor. This set of towels was a perfect remedy for troubled times!

Towel patterns on pages 72-75

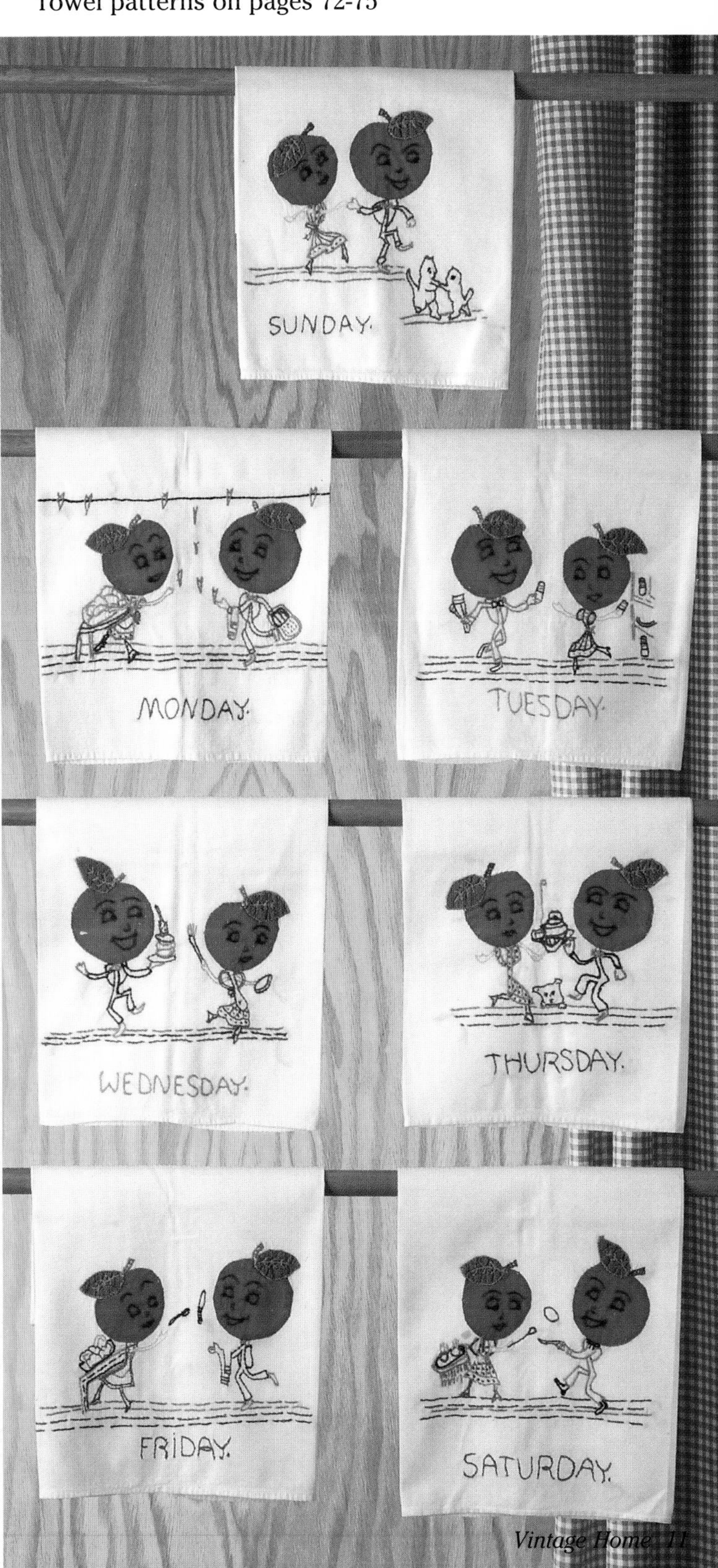

Daily Dishes

A dish a day and pretty soon you've stitched right through the week. Charming redwork embroidery adds color and cheer to any kitchen.

Towel patterns on pages 68-71.

Woman's Weekly

This girl is on the go, a Forty's girl if there ever was one. Clever "chore" towels show her working and having fun. Add a set of these towels to your kitchen... they'll make you smile every day!

The practice of assigning a task to each day of the week on a towel was immensely popular. Beginning in the 1920's and continuing today, it's the one aspect of "art needlework" which has not fallen off.

Whether embroidered, tinted, or painted, the towels continue to be decorated. Most sets of "chore" towels either had six of the major chores or had seven towels and included a restful Sunday activity, usually church.

The chores invariably included: cleaning, washing, ironing, baking, marketing, sewing, and rest or church on Sunday.

Towel patterns on pages 48-51.

The style and fashions are vintage WW2 homefront. This gal even wears her skirts shorter than her Thirties counterparts to comply with wartime rationing and fabric availability. What a trooper!

Quilt patterns on pages 52-57.

A bit of fun,
A touch of mirth
Helps brighten up the day -
It often makes the work we do
Seem a bit like play!

Modern Woman

This woman has her hands full. She's both sophisticated and handy (pardon the broken china!). And check out her favorite saying around the border, "A man works from sun to sun... a woman's work is never done".

Finish off the quilt with the perfect border... fabric picturing kitchen appliances that make life easier for women in the home.

Women and Men

Poking fun at the opposite sex was one thing designers loved to do and a theme women loved to stitch. These pillowslips from the 1950's are a great example of this trend. If men ran the world, women certainly had the last word on it.

Pillowcase patterns on pages 76-77.

Fun in the Kitchen

Once again active cookware works its magic on towels. The kitchen never settles down. The combination of traditional sayings enacted by dishes is total magic.

Dishes, utensils, and household items were busy everywhere. It must have been wishful thinking that these things could get their work done by themselves while the ladies took a bit of leisure!

Towel patterns on pages 78-81.

Help in the Kitchen

Men in the kitchen, what's next?

Well, it turns out they start to show up all over the house and around the yard as well.

Beginning in the late 1930's and continuing into the 1940's, couples doing chores was very popular. This adorable tinted couple - Mrs. and "Butterfingers" - was typical of the clumsy husband theme.

They loved to help, but was it worth it? Men breaking dishes was probably the most popular situation stitched on towels.

Pattern on pages 82-83.

Dancing in the Kitchen

If the guy helping happened to be a butler, well - you were a lucky person. This combination of maid and butler was one that began to disappear in the Forties. The war created a vast number of high paying jobs in factories and quickly drained the pool of domestic help that was available.

Pattern on pages 84-85.

Chefs like to prance
nose in the air,
One wonders what's
to see up there.

Dancing Chef Apron pattern on pages 34-35.
Chef with Cake Towel pattern on page 86.
Green Woman in the Kitchen pattern on page 36.
Green Chef in the Kitchen pattern on page 37.

A Chef in the Kitchen

The chef was almost always chubby as was the maid shapely. This rule holds true on this page as well.

This selection of men trying their hand at cooking is a wonderful assortment typifying needlework humor. From the sausage stealing pooch to the parading chef, these are some great designs for perking up your kitchen.

Some of these designs are a combination of applique and embroidery. This was very popular in the Thirties and Forties and is a totally adorable mixture.

Little bits of fabric anchoring the picture has an enchanting effect.

Quilt square patterns on pages 87-89.

Hot Pads and Potholders

Call them 'potholders' or 'hot pads' - if you cook, you need them. You might as well have a chuckle, too.

Decorative potholders were a perennial favorite in the needle and fancy work catalogs from the 1910's up until today. One has to have these in the kitchen, therefore it follows that they must be decorated.

Every needlework catalog in the Thirties and Forties had at least one page, if not two of potholder kits. Tinting was used in a lot of these. Sets often included anywhere from two to three hotpads and some kind of pocket or hanging rack for storage.

These coordinated pads and potholders created charming little vignettes to hang on the walls. They are still coveted by collectors and are a favorite decoration in vintage linen enthusiasts' homes.

Pots and Pans Potholder patterns on pages 90-93.

Waitress and Chef Potholder patterns on page 19.

Waitress and Chef Potholders

Photo on page 18

TINTING instructions on page 81

Woman's Work

Photo on page 3

TINTING instructions on page 81

Housework seems to never end
We work the whole day through,
One would think eventually
We'd nothing left to do.

'China' Exercising

Photo on page 4

Appropriate it seems to send
A pillow to so close a friend.
It's filled with grateful thoughts of you,
Oh yes, of course, some feathers too!

McCall Decorative Arts
and Needlework
Winter, 1928

'China' Dancing

Photo on page 4

Lady in a Bowl

Photo on page 5

TINTING instructions on page 81

I don't care how funny I look. My kids think I'm a swinging cook!

Serving Cake

Photo on page 5

My beau's coming over to dinner.
I like it when he comes a-calling.
I sure do hope this cake's a winner -
At least I kept the thing from falling!

Laundry on a Windy Day

Photo on page 6

TINTING instructions on page 81

Enlarge the laundry tree pattern 150% to measure 6" x 16".

It's a really pretty day,
Clear and downright sunny!
Should I whistle while I work
Or hum a song that's funny?

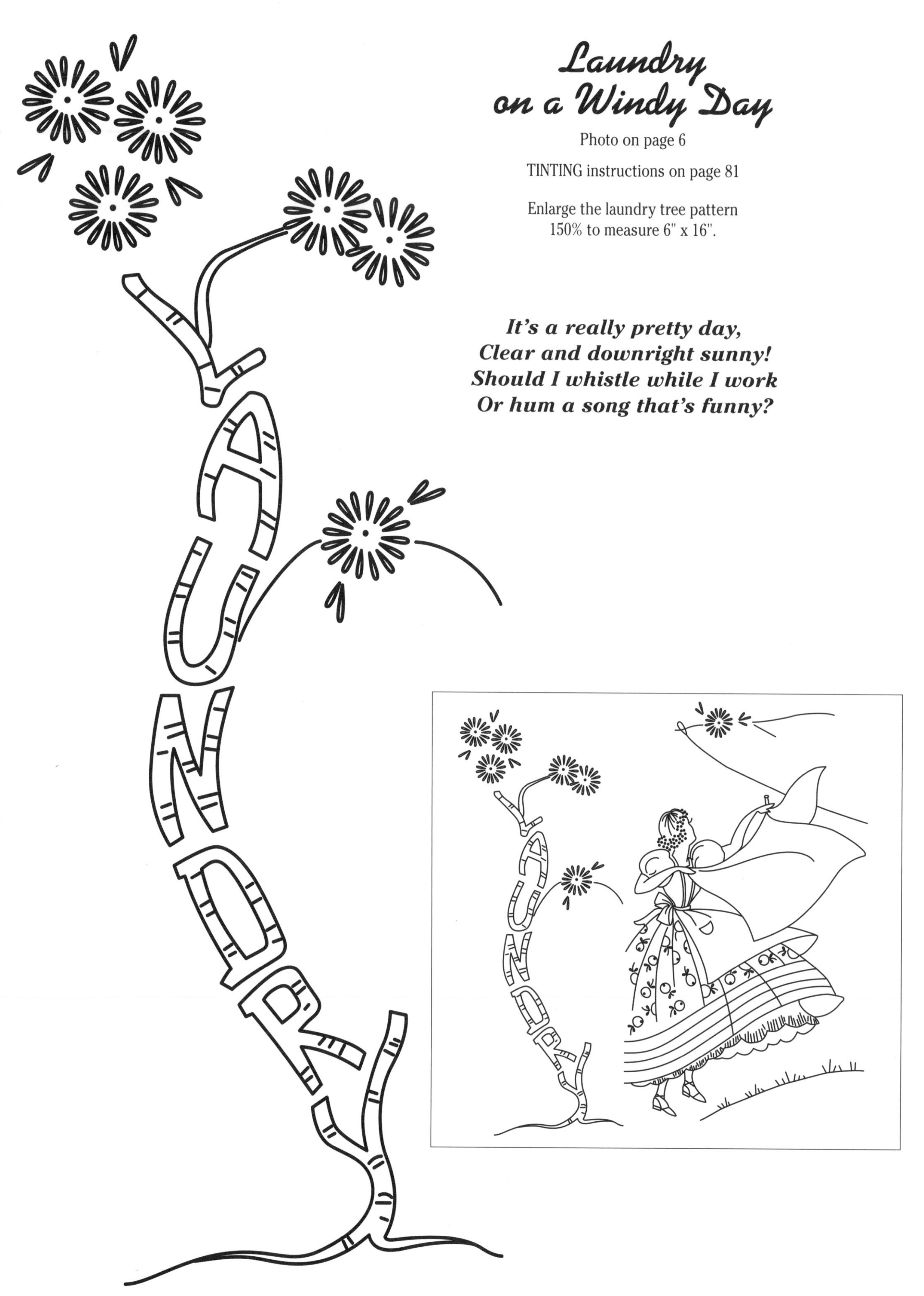

There's always so much work to do,
I work every day and never fret.
Bake bread, clean the house,
cook some stew
Washed all day and
I'm not done yet!

Bonnet Babe with Laundry

Photo on page 7

TINTING instructions on page 81

Laundry on a Windy Day

Photo on page 6

TINTING instructions on page 81

Enlarge the laundry tree pattern 120% to measure 10" x 16".

Of all the chores I do around here
I mostly like to do the laundry.
Soak, scrub and rinse to remove each stain.
Day in, day out and year after year.

But on some days I get overcome
And there's something else that bothers me -
Where does all this laundry come from?
The stuff surely must grow on a tree!

Piles of laundry are like a book, Each stain and spot tells a story. What do kids do? Just take a look. They're living life in all its glory!

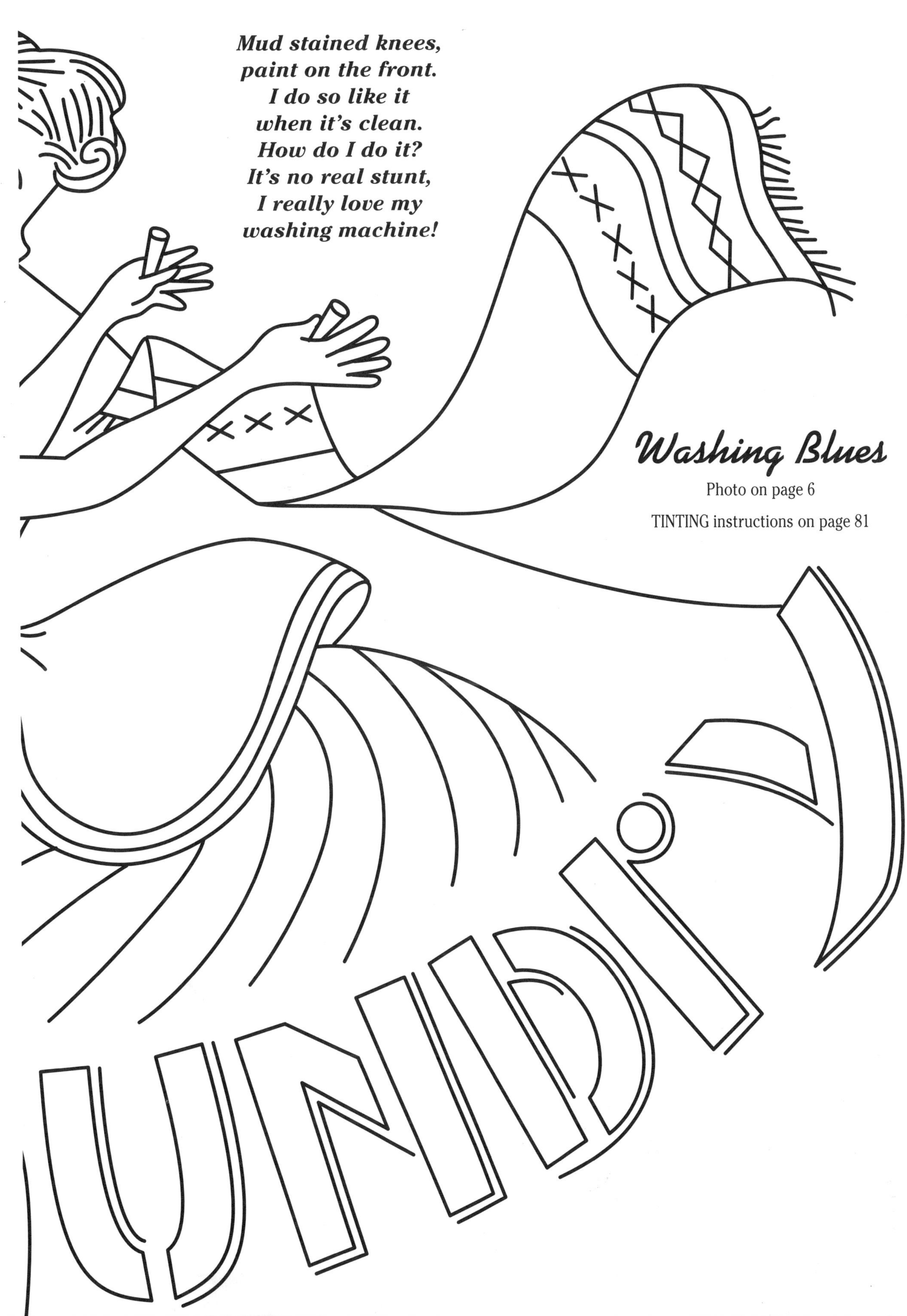

Mud stained knees,
paint on the front.
I do so like it
when it's clean.
How do I do it?
It's no real stunt,
I really love my
washing machine!

Washing Blues

Photo on page 6

TINTING instructions on page 81

Apron

Photo on page 2

I love to cook
And I love to clean.
Every day I do my chores,
It's what I do for hours.

But on some days,
Not all days, I mean.
I'd love to take a walk outside
And maybe pick some flowers!

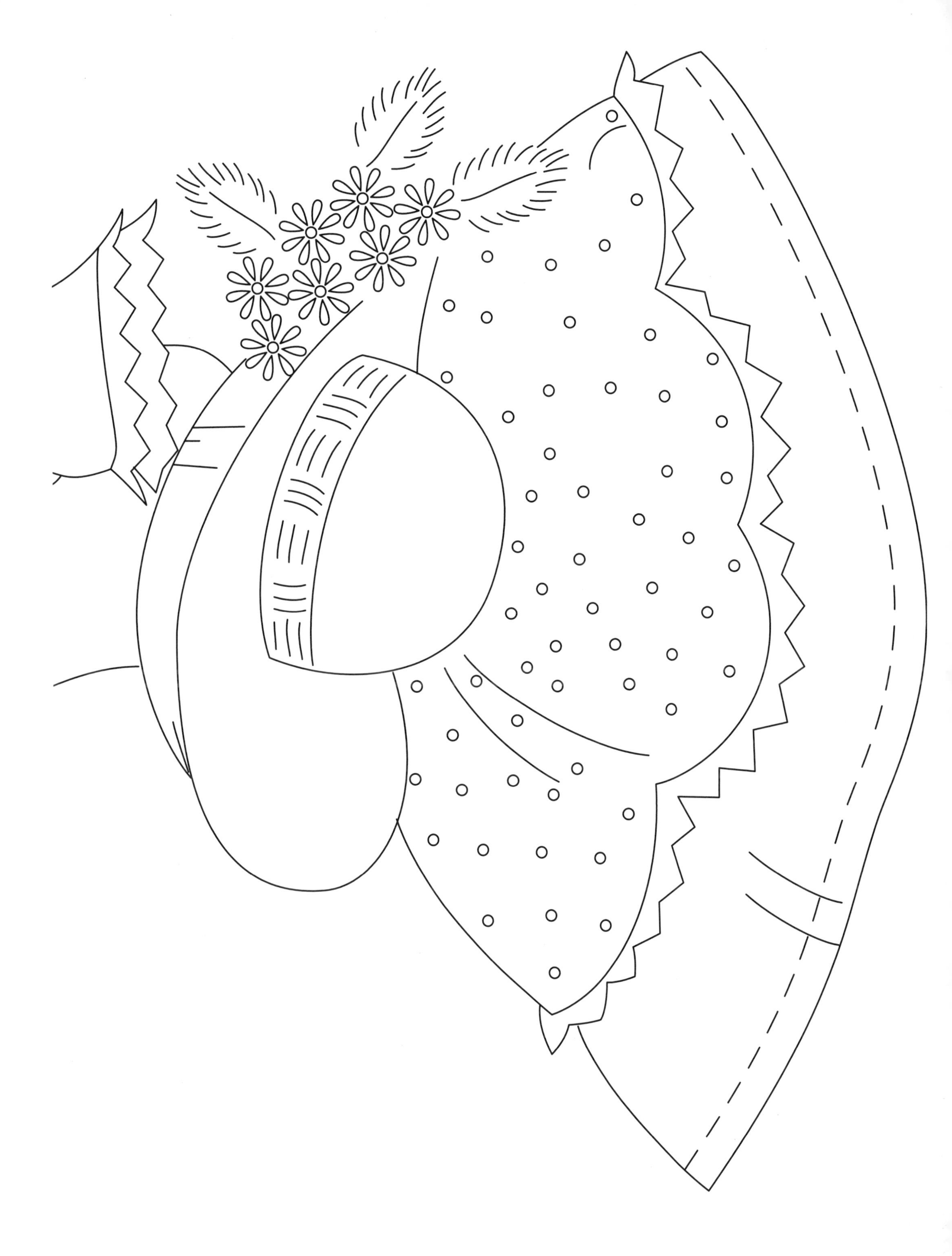

Dancing Chef

Photo on page 16

A married couple prospers
When both help with the chores
Even if it's she inside
And he works out of doors.

Green Woman in the Kitchen

Photo on page 16

Dancing across the floor with this tray,
May not be anybody's favorite way
To earn a living, to make ends meet,
But I chose to do work on my feet!

Heirloom Linens Care

As vintage linens have become more collectible, many enthusiasts have become textile conservators to their own mini-museums of heirloom dresser scarves, doilies and Day-of-the-week towels.

It isn't hard or expensive to store and clean your collection safely, if you take advantage of some common sense - and some new products.

Roll linens to prevent ironing them!

Rolling linens for storage, like Grandma did, was so widely practiced that embroidery kits for decorative linen rolls were popular sellers in turn-of-the-century catalogs! Today, textile experts heartily endorse Grandma's method. Place a piece of acid-free tissue on the surface of the textile to reduce wrinkles even further. From a practical point of view, rolling may not always be possible. Make sure your most precious linens get this treatment. If you must fold, use acid-free tissue and fold pieces in thirds, not halves. At least creases won't run right through the middle of the piece.

Acid-free cardboard comes to the rescue!

Conservators highly recommend the use of acid-free cardboard to store almost everything - including linens. Why? Air circulation is important to prevent moisture damage - a common culprit in storing textiles. See-through plastic containers, though, are convenient, affordable and available. If you are going to store in plastic, keep the containers away from damp and open them regularly. Indulge in the pleasure of examining your collection often, but wear white cotton gloves to keep from adding moisture from your hands.

Think before you wash - or sink!

Conservators view washing as a last resort for restoring the look of linens. Simply airing textiles to remove musty smells is far safer than washing will ever be - and it's definitely the first step to try. Never use a new, untried product on a treasured heirloom! Instead, try the product out on a few "disposable" vintage scraps to test its stain removal abilities first.

Modern science in the kitchen cupboard!

Many antique dealers and quilt shops carry stain removers formulated especially to remove age spots from antique linens. Homemade formulas abound, as well. A solution of equal parts Biz and Cascade has many loyal users, as does baking soda and lemon juice. Remember that washing is only half the battle - rinsing is equally important, since detergent residue actually attracts dirt and oil to fibers. After rinsing, smooth the article carefully on a towel and roll gently to press out moisture. Never, ever wring an heirloom textile item! Lay the piece flat to dry, unless you really don't care if the item is permanently stretched out of shape.

Harness the sun for good - not evil!

Mildew stains can be bleached somewhat from white linens by washing them and drying them flat in sunshine. But beware! Direct sunlight is guaranteed to fade any colored textile or embroidery. If your heart is set on cafe curtains from old printed tablecloths, resign yourself to seeing their bright colors fade over time. Glass and sunlight are another combination that textile guardians caution against. A good framer knows to recommend plexiglass or a glass that screens ultraviolet rays when framing your heirloom embroidery.

Green Chef in the Kitchen

Photo on page 16

Since I was a lad at my mother's knee,
I knew exactly what I wanted to be.
I wanted to cook, saute and stew
Lovely meals to appeal just to you!

Embroidery Stitches

Separate embroidery floss. - Use 24" lengths of floss in a #8 embroidery needle. Use 2 to 3 ply floss to outline large elements of the design and to embroider larger and more stylized patterns. Use 2 strands for the small details on some items.

Drawing Stitches

Use these stitches to work along the lines of the designs.

Back Stitch -

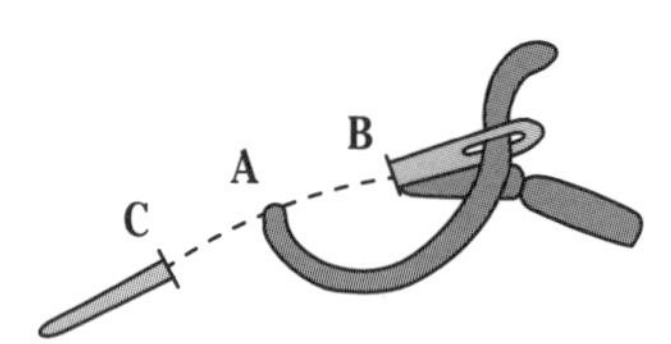

Come up at A, go down at B. Come back up at C. Repeat.

Stem Stitch -

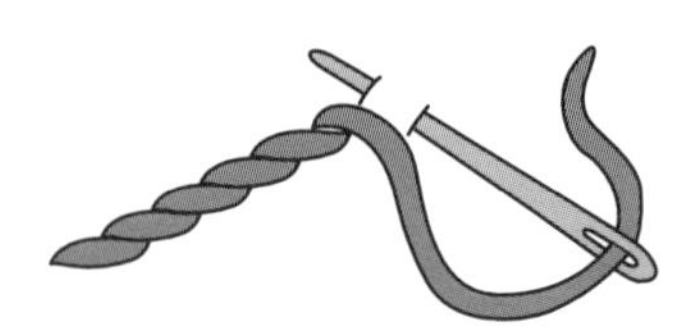

Work from left to right to make regular, slanting stitches along the stitch line. Bring the needle up above the center of the last stitch. Also called "Outline" stitch.

Straight Stitch -

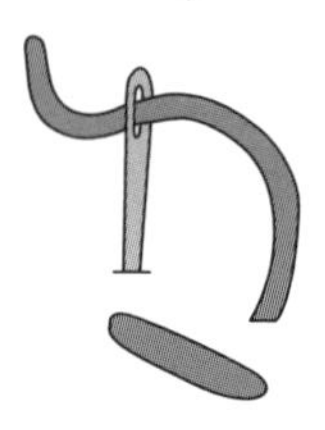

Come up at A and go down at B to form a simple flat stitch. Use this stitch for hair for animals and for simple petals on small flowers.

Lazy Daisy Stitch -

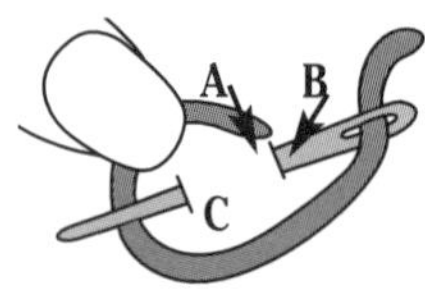

Come up at A, go down at B (next to A) to form a loop. Come back up at C with needle tip over the thread. Go down at D to make a small anchor stitch over the top of the loop. Use this stitch for petals of larger flowers.

Running Stitch -

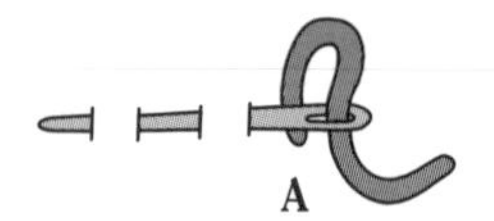

Come up at A. Weave the needle through the fabric, making short, even stitches. Use this stitch to gather fabrics, too.

Filling Stitch

Use this stitch to fill in colored areas of the designs.

Satin Stitch -

Work small Straight stitches close together and at the same angle to fill an area with stitches. Vary the length of the stitches as required to keep the outline of the area smooth.

Pay attention to backgrounds. - When working with lighter-colored fabrics, do not carry dark flosses across large unworked background areas. Stop and start again to prevent unsightly "ghost strings" from showing through from the front.

Decorative Stitches

Use these stitches to embellish areas of the designs.

Cross Stitch -

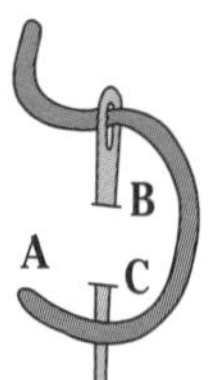

Make a diagonal Straight stitch (up at A, down at B) from upper right to lower left. Come up at C and go down at D to make another diagonal Straight stitch the same length as the first one. The stitch will form an X.

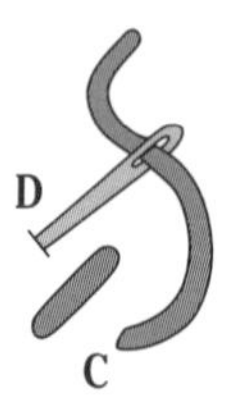

French Knot -

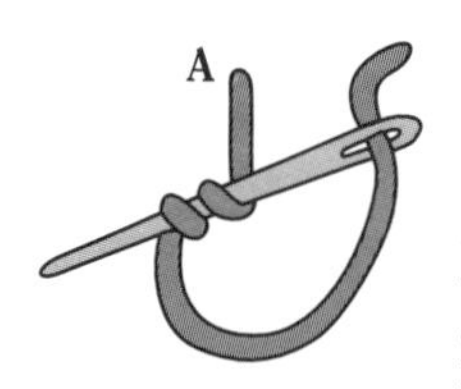

Come up at A. Wrap the floss around the needle 2 - 3 times. Insert the needle close to A. Hold the floss and pull the needle through the loops gently.

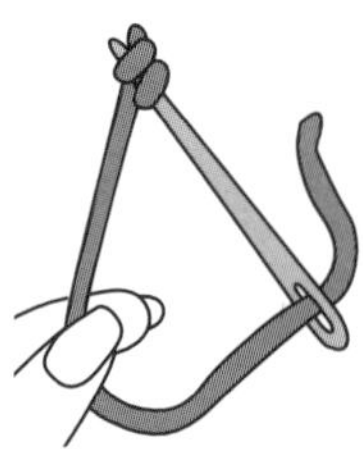

Feather Stitch -

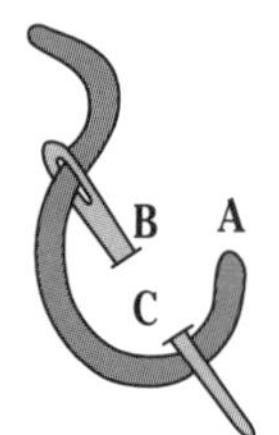

Come up at A, go down at B (to the left of A). Come back up at C with needle tip of thread to form a V. Alternate stitches from side to side. Use this stitch for the veins of large leaves or petals.

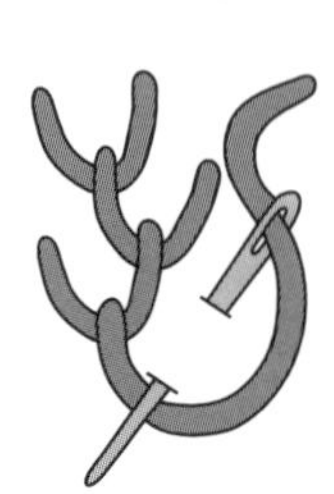

Edging Stitches

Use these stitches to finish edges of projects.

Blanket Stitch -

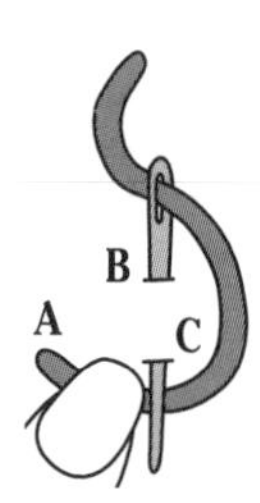

Come up at A, hold the thread down with your thumb, go down at B. Come back up at C with the needle tip over the thread. Pull the stitch into place. Repeat, outlining with the bottom legs of the stitch. Use this stitch to edge fabrics.

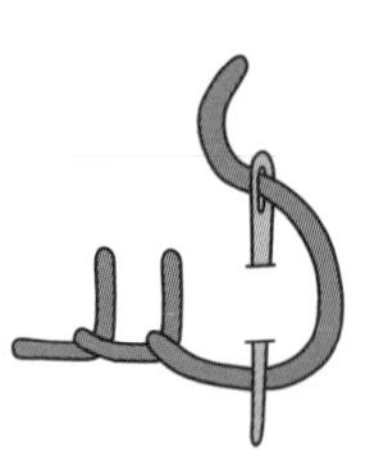

Whip Stitch -

Insert the needle under a few fibers of one layer of fabric. Bring the needle up through the other layer of fabric. Use this stitch to attach the folded raw edges of fabric to the back of pieces or to attach bindings around the edges of quilts and coverlets.

Basic Alphabet for Quick Embroidery

ABCDEFGHIJ
KLMNOPQRS
TUVWXYZ
abcdefghijklmn
opqrstuvwxyz

Dirty Bird

Photo on page 7

I'm glad that mine's a small place,
There's not a lot of room.
It's small, so I don't make a face
When I sweep it with a broom!

"I Woke and Found That Life Was Duty"

Photo on page 8

Enlarge the pattern 140% to measure 14" x 20".

If I lived in a big home,
A lot more work would loom.
And with all that room to roam,
I'd really need a vacuum!

Mammy with Cake

Photo on page 8

TINTING instructions on page 81

I woke up early,
without an alarm,
It's my special day, for
heaven's sake!
My duty is to turn
on the charm
While they all sing over
my birthday cake!

Repeat BORDER at the bottom of design

4 Mammy Designs

Photo on page 9

I work the garden at morning hours -
What's that thing on the ground I see?
It's hiding underneath the flowers.
I'll be! I see a pesky ol' weed!

4 Mammy Designs

Photo on page 9

I'm wishing to myself as I dust,
While I am standing up on this chair,
That this statement all would trust:
"That's no spider web, it's angel hair!"

4 Mammy Designs

Photo on page 9

Long as I live, I do not believe,
There's anything that could ever match
The prettiest sight I can conceive:
A plate stacked high with syrupy flapjacks!

4 Mammy Designs

Photo on page 9

Going about my chores, I have supposed,
I keep on pondering in suspense.
Who told them and who listened to those
Stories that were shared over a fence?

7 Woman's Weekly

Photo on page 12

Last week was long, it's done now.
Our chores we have done already.
To start this week, we make a vow
To stand tall, proud and always steady!

I have always heard it said,
"Women's work is never done."
But I think inside my head,
"Housework is not just for one!"

7 Woman's Weekly

Photo on page 12

I wash the clothes, I press them
And press and stew as I steam.
What's to eat? That thought is grim.
A dinner out! That's my dream!

Thing get old and they wear out.
Darn and stitch, I have to mend.
But at times I want to shout,
"Why doesn't it ever end?!?"

7 Woman's Weekly

Photo on page 12

Go out and do the shopping.
Get eggs, bread, milk, cheese and ham.
These errands keep me hopping -
And the grocer called me "Ma'am!"

Housework is just so boring.
Cleaning? Goodness! It's a heap!
But I attack it, I am roaring!
Look at this! I made a clean sweep!

Care of Linens

Washing -

• Test for colorfastness on the seam allowance. Let several drops of water fall through the fabric onto white blotter paper. If color appears, the fabric is not colorfast.

• To set dye, soak fabric in water and vinegar.

• Wash with a very mild detergent or soap, using tepid water. Follow all label instructions carefully.

• Do not use chlorine bleach on fine linen. Whiten it by hanging it in full sunlight.

Stain Removal -

• Grease - Use a presoak fabric treatment and wash in cold water.

• Nongreasy - Soak in cold water to neutralize the stain. Apply a presoak and then wash in cold water.

• Ballpoint Ink - Place on an absorbent material and soak with denatured or rubbing alcohol. Apply room temperature glycerin and flush with water. Finally, apply ammonia and quickly flush with water.

• Candle Wax - Place fabric between layers of absorbent paper and iron on low setting. Change paper as it absorbs wax. If a stain remains, wash with peroxide bleach.

• Rust - Remove with lemon juice, oxalic acid or hydrofluoric acid.

Storage -

• Wash and rinse thoroughly in soft water.

• Do not size or starch.

• Place cleaned linen on acid-free tissue paper and roll loosely.

• Line storage boxes with a layer of acid-free tissue paper.

• Place rolled linens in a box. Do not stack. Weight causes creases.

• Do not store linens in plastic bags.

• Hang linen clothing in a muslin bag or cover with a cotton sheet.

7 Woman's Weekly

Photo on page 12

I pay attention to what I eat.
I really follow a good diet.
After eating good all week,
I must indulge! Just try it!

6 'Modern' Women

Photo on page 13

I don't know much about physical laws. Those things don't mean a lot to me. But there are times when I do take pause And wish there were no law of gravity!

Modern Women Quilt

This little quilt is a humorous reminder for today's modern woman, that yesteryear women wore heels and pearls to do chores. Say, "Hooray for progress!"

FINISHED SIZE: 58" x 44"

MATERIALS:
- 44" wide, 100% cotton fabrics:
  - 1 yard of muslin for blocks and sashing
  - 3/4 yard of Gold print for filler blocks,
  - 1 yard of Green print for border
  - 1 1/2 yards for backing
- 6 yards of Black 3/4" double fold bias binding
- 52" x 66" piece of quilt batting
- Assorted embroidery flosses
- Scraps of assorted fabrics for applique.
- pins • thread • needle • scissors

CUTTING:
- DESIGN BLOCKS:
  Cut 6 muslin 10 1/2" x 10 1/2" squares
- FILLER BLOCKS:
  Cut 5 Gold print 10 1/2" x 10 1/2" squares
  Cut 2 Gold print 7 1/2" x 7 1/2" squares
  Cut 4 Gold print 6 1/2" x 6 1/2" squares
- SASHING:
  Cut 2 muslin 2 1/2" x 28 1/2" strips.
  Cut 2 muslin 2 1/2" x 47" strips.

BORDERS:
  Cut 4 Green 6 1/4" x 20 1/2" strips.
  Cut 4 Green 6 1/4" x 19 1/2" strips
- BACKING;
  Cut 2 muslin 26 1/2" x 66" pieces

DESIGN BLOCKS:

Trace the designs on page 52 - 57 to the center of the design blocks, referring to the photo on page 13. Place designs on the blocks 'on point.'

Trace the words on the muslin borders from the pillow pattern on page 20. Embroider words.

Embroider and applique designs and words. Press each design.

APPLIQUE:

To applique designs, cut fabric pieces 1/4" larger than the shape around all edges. Fold back and press the seam allowance, clipping curves as necessary. Use matching thread to whip stitch the edges of the fabric in place around the outline of the shape.

Place designs "on point."

ASSEMBLY:

1. Use 1/4" seam allowances throughout.

2. Cut 3 of the filler blocks in half, point to point. With right sides facing, sew a filler block half at the sides of one of the design blocks, as shown in the illustration. Sew another design block and a filler block together. Repeat with another design block, then a filler block half. Use the same method to sew the remaining design block, filler block and filler block halves together to form diagonal rows. Press seams toward the filler blocks and halves.

continued on page 54

I wish - and I wish it every day,
(Believe me, this is a household must!)
That some smart person on some fine day,
Will find a permanent cure for dust!

6 'Modern' Women

Photo on page 13

6 'Modern' Women

Photo on page 13

I've scoured the house
and now I have guests.
I've scrubbed and dusted,
I am the queen!
Now I feel I must
serve them my best.
But after they've gone?
I get to clean!

continued from pages 52-53

3. Cut the $7\frac{1}{2}$"corner blocks in half, point to point. With right sides facing, sew the corner triangles to the remaining side of the corner design blocks.

4. With right sides facing, sew the muslin sashing strips in place. Press the seams toward the border strips.

5. With right sides facing, sew the muslin top and bottom sashing strips in place. Trim ends even. Press seams toward the border strips.

6. With right sides facing, sew a Green top border strip to one side of a $6\frac{1}{2}$" Gold border square. Sew another Green top border to the other side of the square. Press seams open. Repeat for the bottom border. With right sides facing, sew the top border strips in place. Trim ends even. Press the seams toward the border strips.

7. Sew the Green side border strips and Gold border blocks together in the same manner. Sew borders in place. Trim ends even. Press seams toward the border strips.

8. With right sides facing, sew the backing pieces together along the long edges. Press seam open.

9. Layer the backing, batting and the assembled top to form a sandwich. Center the top on the batting. Baste the layers together.

10. Quilt as desired.

11. Remove the basting stitches. Trim the backing and batting even with the edges of the quilt top.

12. Bind the edges with Black bias binding. With right sides facing, sew strip ends together. Press seams open. With right sides facing, sew strips to front of quilt, fold back $\frac{1}{4}$" over the raw edge. Fold over, whip stitch folded edge in place on the

Out taking a walk in my new dress.
Hope I catch the eye of a fella!
I'm quite a cutie, I must confess!
But who sees me under an umbrella?!?

6 'Modern' Women

Photo on page 13

6
'Modern' Women

Photo on page 13

Alas and alack! What can I bake?
Unexpected guests are due at six.
Surely I can't go wrong with a cake!
I hope they can't tell I used a mix!

6 'Modern' Women

Photo on page 13

'Twas a busy day the whole day long.
What's a woman to do in a spin?
She takes a breath, she does no wrong.
When she decides to cook a chicken!

7 Kitchen Mates

Photo on page 10

My sweetheart is a real cut-up,
A comic, a wit and a clown.
He's free-spirited, always "up"
He lifts me up when I'm down!

She is such a little cutie,
And she's always in a rush.
When I walk with the lovely beauty
That little darlin' makes me blush!

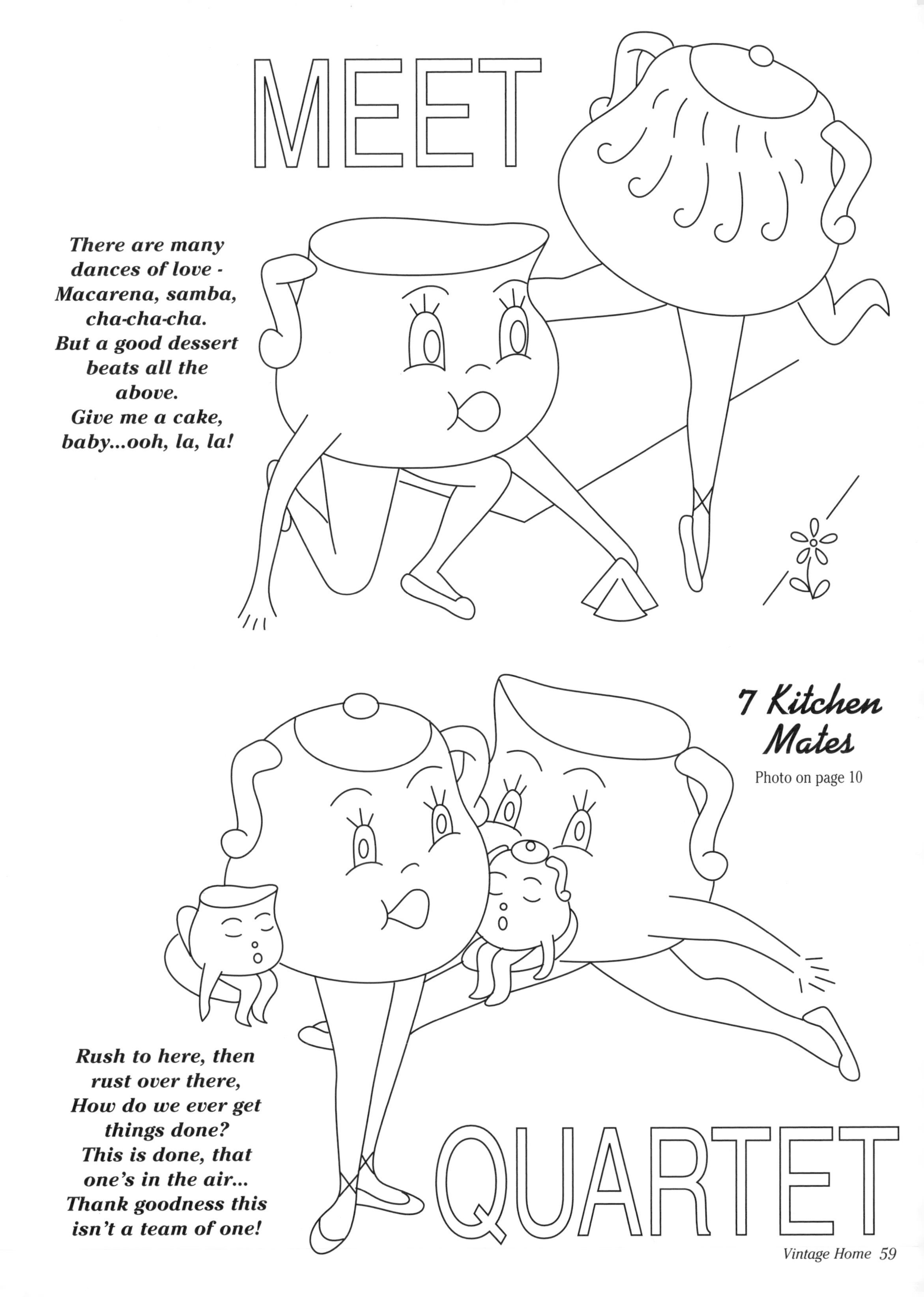
MEET
There are many dances of love - Macarena, samba, cha-cha-cha. But a good dessert beats all the above. Give me a cake, baby...ooh, la, la!
7 Kitchen Mates
Photo on page 10
Rush to here, then rust over there, How do we ever get things done? This is done, that one's in the air... Thank goodness this isn't a team of one!
QUARTET

Photo on page 10

7 Kitchen Mates

Photo on page 10

I love life with my blushing bride,
She takes excellent care of me.
She's the source of my daily pride
Her love for me keeps me in rhapsody!

6 Ladies at Home

Photo on page 10

Work hard, then celebrate!
Bake a berry pie.
Rewards won't be late,
Tell your woes good-bye!!

6 Ladies at Home

Photo on page 10

I'll sweep the doormat,
I like the doorstep clean.
When I'm done with that?
The cleanest porch you've seen!

6 Ladies at Home

Photo on page 10

I just cleaned this floor!
Where'd this dirt come from?
I know when to do this chore:
After the doggie comes home!

6 Ladies at Home

Photo on page 10

The bird's in a snit,
I don't intend to be mean.
The featherduster must be it:
Something he could have been!

6 Ladies at Home

Photo on page 10

Pour a cup of tea,
And bake a cake or two.
Sit with friends and see
Who knows what about who!

6 Ladies at Home

Photo on page 10

Stitch an old saying,
Hang it up real high.
Read it every evening
And follow it - or try!

7 Daily Dishes Days of the Week

Photo on page 11

MONDAY
TUESDAY
WEDNESDAY
THURSDAY
FRIDAY SATURDAY

When the guest is on the doorstep, and nothing has gone right

And the family's left the bathroom looking like a perfect fright -

Just you put a little towel on the rack beside the rest,

Then sail down - the perfect hostess - to receive that pesky guest.

- McCall Decorative Arts and Needlework Winter 1928

7 Daily Dishes

Photo on page 11

7 Daily Dishes

Photo on page 11

7 Daily Dishes

Photo on page 11

"Then too, a touch of embroidery work, no matter how small, enhances the beauty of an article and increases its value."
- Art Needlework Catalog Season 1927

7 'Apple a Day'

Photo on page 11

7 *'Apple a Day'*

Photo on page 11

7 'Apple a Day'

Photo on page 11

7 'Apple a Day'

Photo on page 11

SUNDAY THURSDAY
MONDAY FRIDAY
TUESDAY
WEDNESDAY
SATURDAY

Women l

Who knows what is best?
Is it a man or a woman?
And if you fail this simple test?
Answer: There's trouble bloomin'!

the simpler thing

Men

Just as soon as you say,
(You know how it goes)
It's time to call it a day:
This game's over - and you lose!

the important thi

Women and Men

Photo on page 14

n like —

things in life — (MEN)!

like —

things in life — (WOMEN)

3 'Fun in the Kitchen'

Photo on page 14

Who says pots don't work hard?
You just turn on the stove and wait.
But do not let down your guard,
If supper burns, you won't eat at eight!

Stir it up! Mix it up! Hey, hey hey!
Chili, beans, rice and salsa.
What a way to end a day!
Hot tamales, this is good!
Muchas gracias, mi mama!

3 'Fun in the Kitchen'

Photo on page 14

Cooking meals is really a game,
Just like baseball on the TV set.
You whip up batters and bat at flies,
If the meal is good - you've made a hit!

"Let those who will advocate the paper towel for home use, it will be very reluctantly, indeed, and not soon, if ever, that the housewife will discard the dainty linen towels with all their charming possibilities of embroidery in white and color. A clever woman realizes that the towels hanging on the rods in the bathroom are just as much a part of the house decoration as are the draperies in any other room and makes a point of having them as daintily attractive as may be."

- "Modern Priscilla"
October 1915

'Tinting' with Crayons

Crayons Aren't Paints - Even though ironing softens the crayon, their hard nature means that some of the texture of the fabric and the strokes you make will show through - just like when you make a rubbing over a penny. Making your strokes in the same direction can be challenging in large areas, which is why projects with smaller individual areas of color are best suited to crayon tinting.

Tip: Practice on extra muslin first.

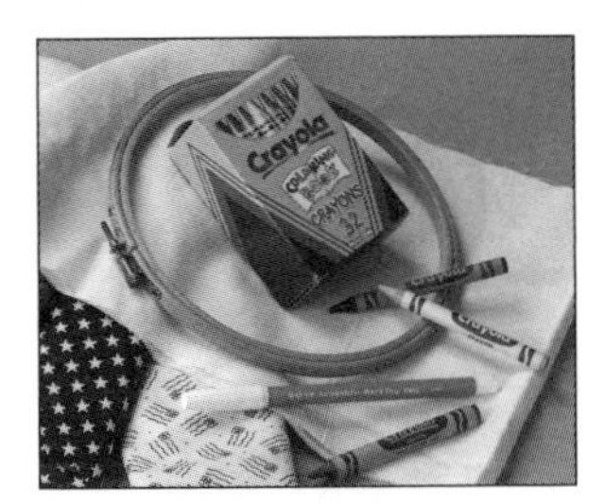

Supplies -
- Muslin fabric
- 24 colors of crayons (or more)
- embroidery floss
- embroidery hoop
- micron pen
- needle

Crayon Hints - Besides being convenient, crayons come in beautiful colors and aren't intimidating. Simply color in the spaces to create the look you want.

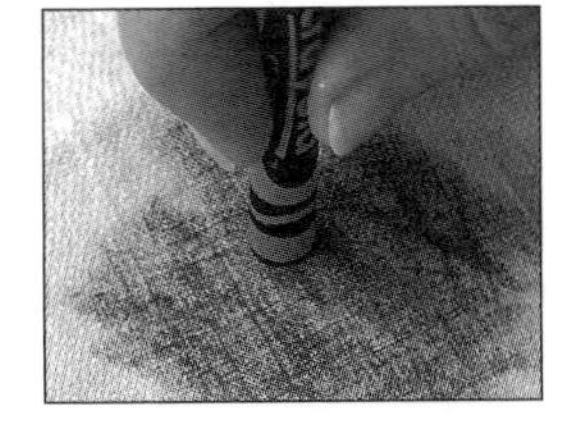

Build Up Color, Edges In

Add layers of crayon color with the strokes going in one direction, or opposite directions for a darker effect. Start lightly - you can always add more. Shading built up from the edges inward helps model or add depth to pieces, so that the tinted areas are not only colorful but three-dimensional as well. You can even choose to leave an area completely open to give a strong highlight.

Use the Correct End

For filling in color, the blunt end of the crayon works best and it works even better if its hard edge is rounded off a little before you start. Keep the pointed end for details or adding a fine shaded line to edges.

Tip: Let the Fabric Do the Work

A shaded fabric (white on white or off white) adds depth to your shading. Larger designs are a little better than fine ones because they give more variety.

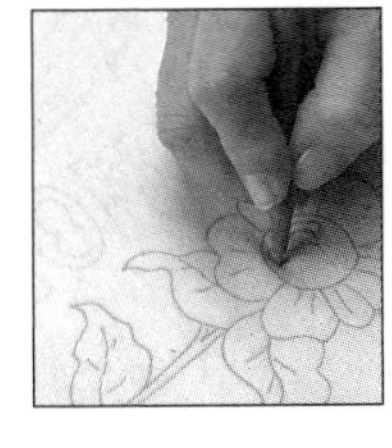

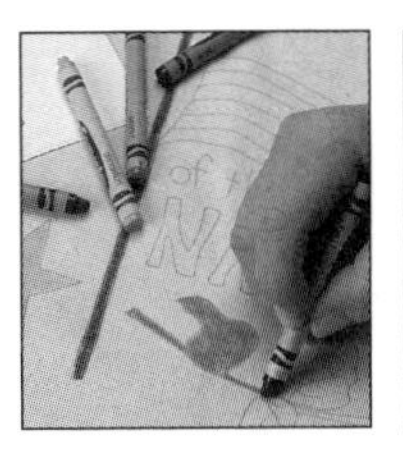

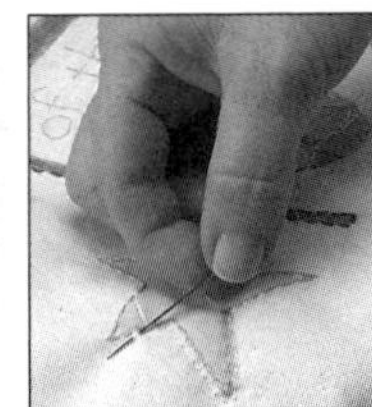

1. Position fabric over a pattern, secure corners with masking tape.

Trace pattern outline directly onto muslin with a blue-line water erase pen or a pencil.

2. Place fabric on a pad of extra fabric and color areas with regular children's crayons.

Color the pattern well with crayon color.

3. Sandwich the fabric between two sheets of plain paper.

Iron on 'cotton' setting to 'set' the crayon colors.

4. If desired, back design with another piece of fabric, place fabric or layers in an embroidery hoop.

Use 3-ply floss to outline the design.

He vowed he would
always love me,
He promised to help
keep the house.
His attempts to help
me are comedy!
Who is this man,
my loving spouse?

Help in the Kitchen

Photo on page 15

TINTING instructions on page 81

I made a stew for the privileged few.
And now I need your approval.
If I were you, I'd love the stew,
Or I foresee your removal!

Dancing in the Kitchen

Photo on page 15

Chef with Cake

Photo on page 16

The lady of the house really relishes,
Entertaining a crowd on her birthday.
But, oh, alas, how can I dare to say,
"Your cherry cake is topped with radishes!"

A Chef in the Kitchen Quilt

Photo on page 17

Even folks who are not big fans of veggies and fruit will get a kick from this little kitchen quilt.

FINISHED SIZE: 27" x 30"

MATERIALS:

- 44" wide, 100% cotton fabrics:
  - 3/8 yard of Red/White check for border
  - 1/4 yard of Blue for sashing strips
  - 1/4 yard of White for the design blocks
  - 1 yard for backing
- 4 yards of Red 3/4" bias binding
- 35" x 38" piece of quilt batting
- Assorted embroidery flosses
- pins • thread • needle • scissors

CUTTING:

- Cut 6 White 6 1/2" x 6 1/2" squares for the top and bottom rows of design blocks
- Cut 3 White 6 1/2" x 9 1/2" squares for the center row of design blocks
- Cut 4 Blue 1 1/2" x 6 1/2" strips for the vertical sashing strips on the top and bottom rows.
- Cut 2 Blue 1 1/2" x 9 1/2" strips for the vertical sashing strips on the center row.
- Cut 2 Blue 1 1/2" x 20 1/2" strips for the horizontal sashing strips
- Cut 2 Blue 1 1/2" x 23 1/2" strips for the side sashing.
- Cut 2 Blue 21 1/2" x 22 1/2" strips for the top and bottom sashings.
- Cut 2 Red/White check 2 3/4" x 25 1/2" strips for the side borders.
- Cut 2 Red/White check 2 3/4" x 27 1/2" strips for the top and bottom borders.
- Cut a a 35" x 38" piece for backing.

DESIGN BLOCKS:

Transfer the designs on page 87 - 89 to the center of the design blocks, referring to the photo on page 17. Embroider designs and words. Press each design.

continued on page 88

A Chef in the Kitchen Quilt

Photo on page 17

ASSEMBLY:

TIP: Use 1/4" seam allowances throughout.

1. With right sides facing, sew a 6 1/2" sashing strip between two 6 1/2" design blocks. Sew another short sashing strip and 6 1/2" design block to one end. Repeat with the remaining 6 1/2" squares and sashing strips. Use the same method to sew the 9 1/2" blocks and sashing strips together. Press seams open.

2 With right sides facing, sew the top row of 6 1/2" blocks to one of the 20 1/2" Blue sashing strips. Sew the center row of 9 1/2" blocks to the other side of the sashing strip. Repeat to add another sashing strip and the bottom row of design blocks. Press seams open.

3. With right sides facing, sew the Blue side sashing strips in place. Trim ends even. Press the seams toward the border strips.

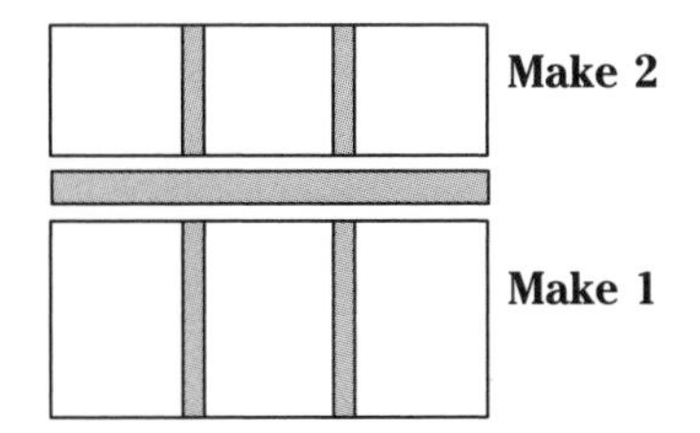

4. With right sides facing, sew the Blue top and bottom sashing strips in place. Trim ends even. Press seams toward the border strips.

5. With right sides facing, sew the Red/White checked side border strips in place. Trim ends even. Press the seams toward the border strips.

6. With right sides facing, sew the Red/White checked top and bottom border strips in place. Trim ends even. Press seams toward the borders.

7. Layer the backing, batting and the assembled top to form a sandwich. Center the top on the batting. Baste the layers together.

8. Quilt as desired.

9. Remove the basting stitches. Trim the backing and batting even with the edges of the quilt top.

10. Bind the edges with Red 3/4" bias binding. With right sides facing, sew strip ends together. Press seams open. With right sides facing, sew binding to front of quilt, fold back 1/4" over the raw edge. Fold over, whip stitch folded edge in place on the back.

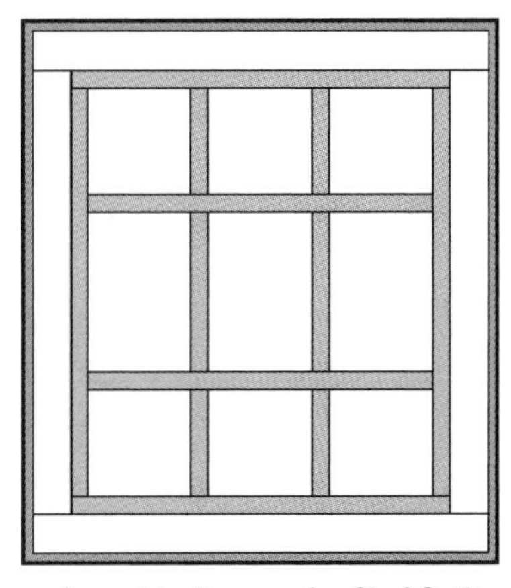

Assembly diagram for Chef Quilt

A Chef in the Kitchen Quilt

Photo on page 17

Potholders -

OPTIONAL :
Tea dye fabric and allow it to dry before making the pieces.

ASSEMBLY:

1. For the half circle holder, shown above, cut a piece of crescent board the same shape as the outline.

2. Cut an 18" x 7" piece of muslin for the front. Transfer design to the center of the fabric and embroider.

3. Center the design over the crescent board and cut the fabric 1/4" larger than the board around all sides. Use the trimmed fabric as a pattern to cut another piece of muslin for the back.

4. Fold the seam allowance on the back piece up over the crescent board. Fold back the seam allowance on the embroidered front and whip stitch the pieces of fabric together around all edges. Finish the edge with double fold bias binding. Attach loop to top center using bias binding.

5. For the potholders on pages 92 and 93, cut an 8" square of cloth for the front of each potholder. Transfer a design to the center of each square. Embroider designs.

6. Center and cut each potholder along the outlines as shown. Reverse and cut a muslin back piece. Cut 2 pieces the same size of either heavy quilt batting or denim for the filling. Sandwich the filling between the 2 pieces of muslin and finish the edge with double fold bias tape.

Whip Stitch -

Insert the needle under a few fibers of one layer of fabric. Bring the needle up through the other layer of fabric. Use this stitch to attach the folded raw edges of fabric to the back of pieces or to attach bindings around the edges of quilts and coverlets.

Pots and Pans

Photo on page 18

TINTING instructions on page 81

Tea Dye Instructions

Dissolve a heaping tablespoon of instant tea per cup of boiling water.

Remove from heat and soak fabric until the desired shade.

Lay fabric out flat and allow to air dry.

Press.

"Without a doubt, homemaking is the most important part of a woman's everyday life - there must be a continual alertness for an idea or a place for a pillow, a runner for a table, a doily for a tray, that fits the place and purpose perfectly and adds just the right emphasis on color and daintiness.

- Art Needlework Catalog Season 1927

Come on, pal, let's go take a stroll.
Let's go over to the doggy park!
Hurry up, pal, we're getting old!
Don't wanna go?
Did you know I bark?

Look at me! I learned to do a trick!
I'm so sweet, and aren't I cute?
What more darling pet could you pick?
Come on, buddy, shake my foot!

Pots and Pans

Photo on page 18

TINTING instructions on page 81

Tea Time Quilt

Photo on page 99

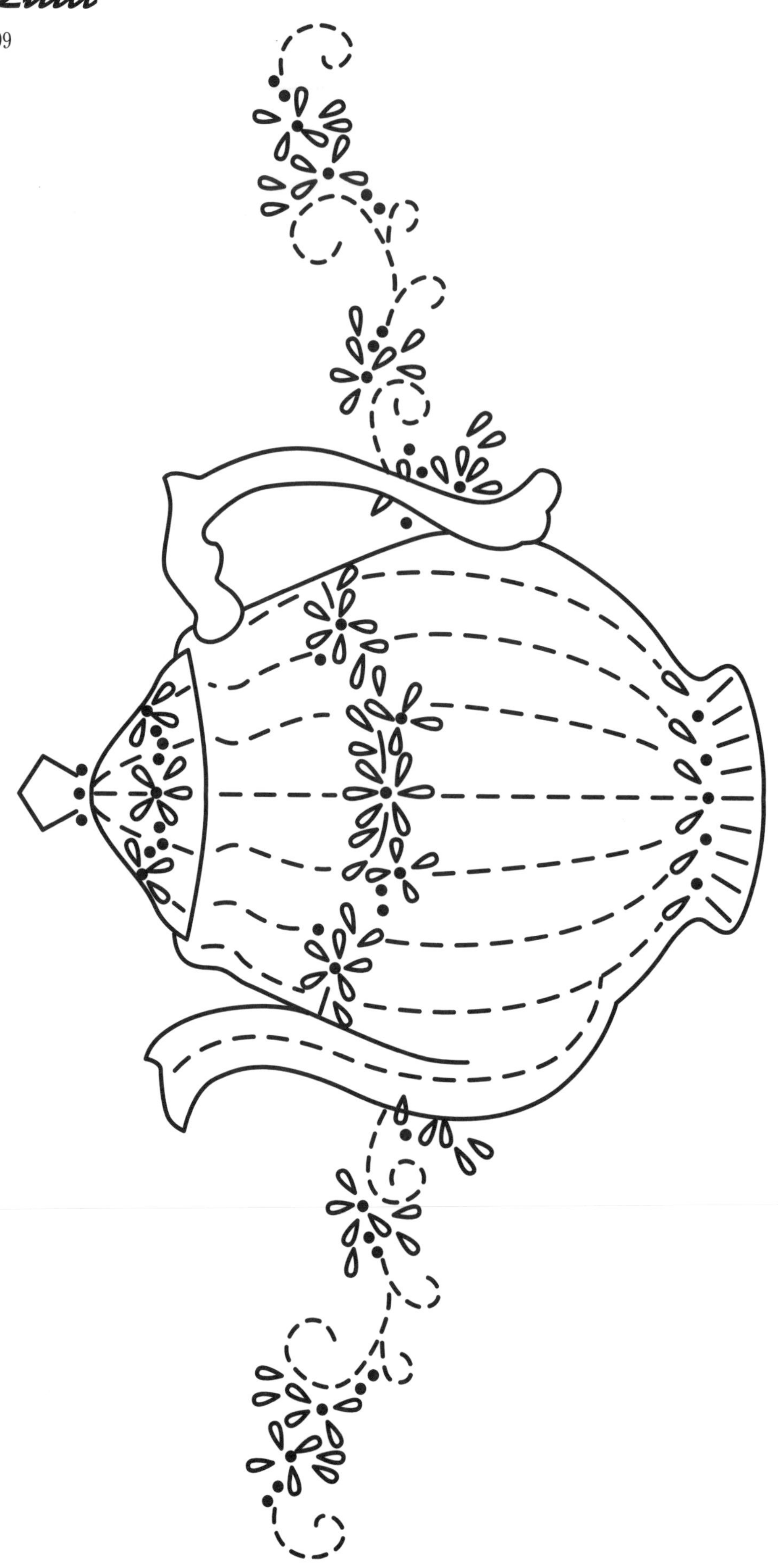

Tea Time Quilt

Photo on page 99

Tea Time Quilt

Photo on page 99

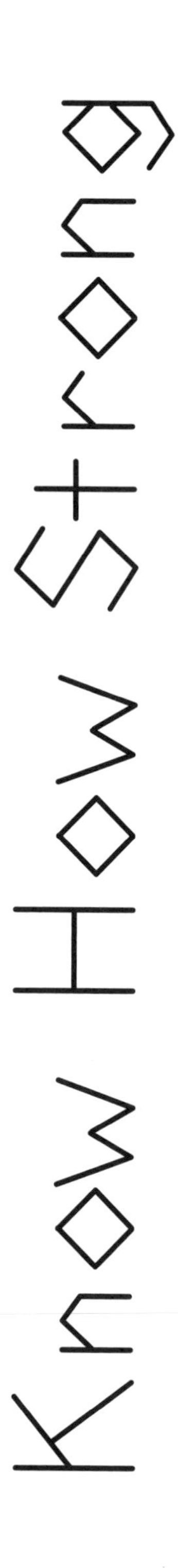

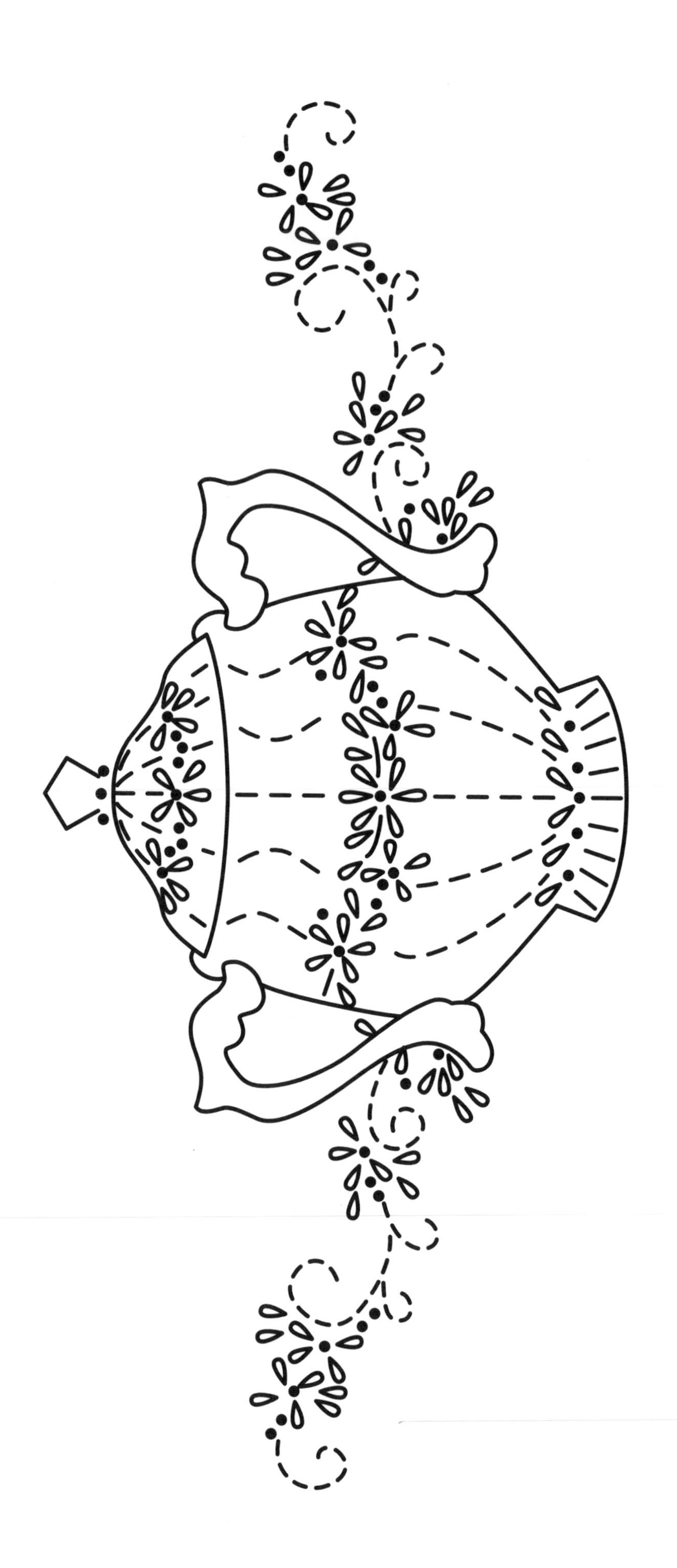

Tea Time Quilt

Photo on page 99

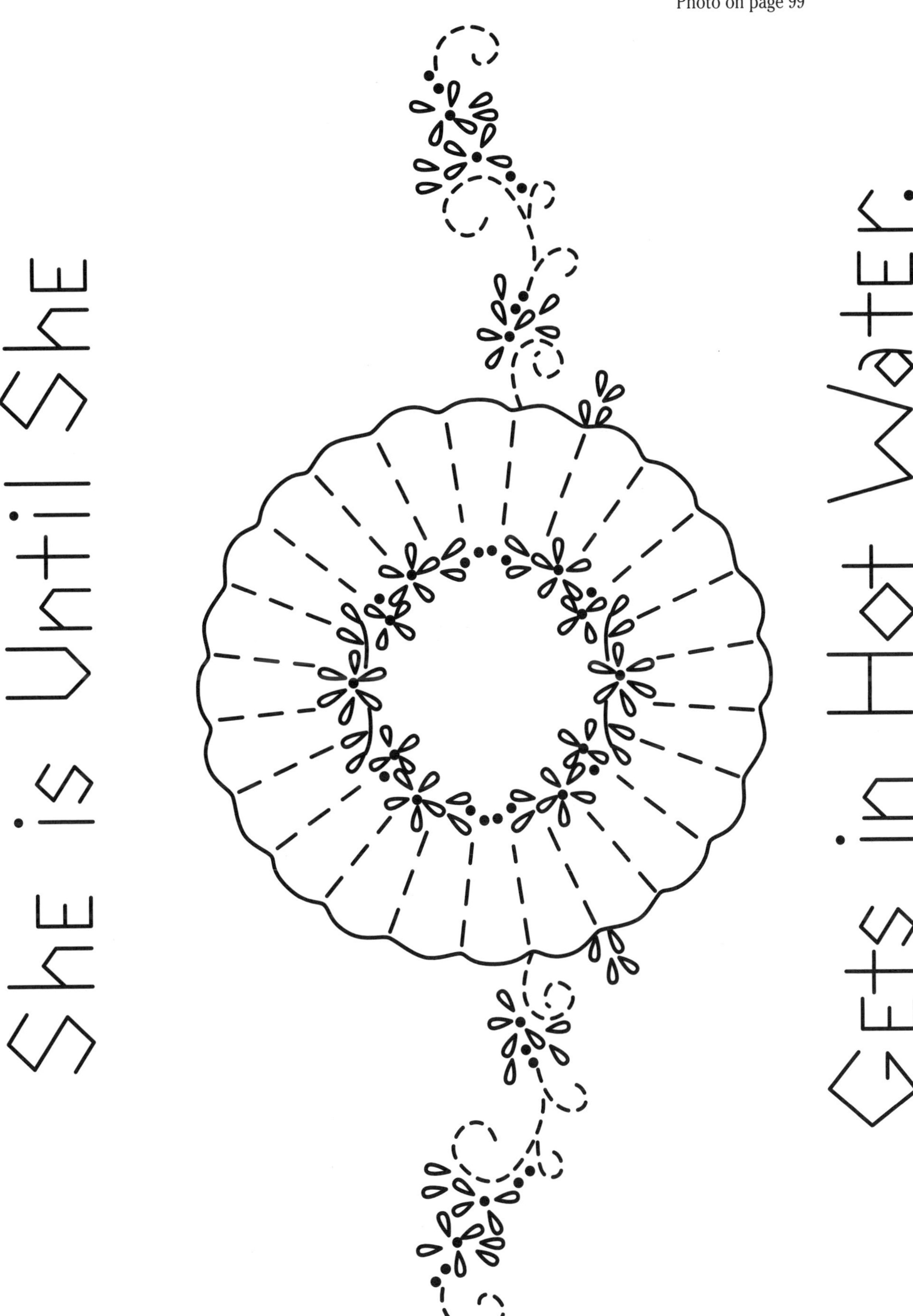

Nori Koenig

I especially love restoring and collecting long-lost embroidery patterns.

The designs featured here are authentic vintage designs. Discovering them took hundreds of hours of handling patterns, reading old catalogs and poring though antique periodicals.

Inherited or collected linens can be a good aid in archiving your family's history. If you are lucky enough to inherit or find a few, be sure to save them... as a link to the past and days gone by.

Nori Koenig

Nori continues to research, restore and collect vintage patterns - all the while making good use of her degrees in history and library science.

A Special Thank You
to Janet Stuart for stitching the wonderful quilts, to Mary Beth Kauffman for restoring antique embroidery and to Charlie Davis Young for her charming poems and verses throughout this book.

Pom Pom Fringe *with a vintage look that is used on pillows in this book is available in several colors from*
The Prym-Dritz Corporation
846-576-5050, Spartanburg, SC

MANY THANKS to my friends for their cheerful help and wonderful ideas!
Kathy McMillan - Jen Tennyson
Charlie Davis Young
Marti Wyble - David & Donna Thomason

How many arrangements,
would you say,
Have been made over
cups of tea?

How many engagements,
business deals,
party plans, vacations or
shopping sprees?

I guess we will never
really know,
But I'd be happy if you'd agree
to have a cup of tea with me!

Who invented all these
things, cups and plates?
What must they have
had in mind?

Who was the first family
to use a dish?
Or fork, or spoon or
knife as they ate?

I guess we will never
really know,
But I'd be happy if you'd agree
to have a nice warm meal with me!

Tea Time Quilt

Design blocks:

Transfer the designs on pages 94 - 97 to the center of the design and word blocks, referring to the photo on page 99. Embroider designs and words. Press each design.

ASSEMBLY:

TIP: Use 1/4" seam allowances throughout.

1. With right sides facing, sew the first word block above the top design block. Sew alternating word and design blocks to the bottom of the first one, following the sequence shown in the photo.

2. With right sides facing, sew the Dark Blue top and bottom inner border strips in place. Trim ends even. Press the seams toward the border strips.

3. With right sides facing, sew the Dark Blue side inner border strips in place. Trim ends even. Press seams toward the border strips.

4. With right sides facing, sew the Light Blue top and bottom border strips in place. Trim ends even. Press the seams toward the border strips.

5. With right sides facing, sew the Light Blue side border strips in place. Trim ends even. Press seams toward the border strips.

6. Layer the backing, batting and the assembled top to form a sandwich. Center the top on the batting. Baste the layers together.

7. Quilt the quilt as desired.

8. Remove the basting stitches. Trim the backing and batting even with the edges of the quilt top.

9. Bind the edges with the Blue 1 1/2" strips. With right sides facing, sew strip ends together. Press seams open. Sew strips to back of quilt, fold back 1/4" along raw edge. Fold over, whip stitch in place.